DATE DUE		

How to Draw
INDIAN
Arts and Crafts

Written and Illustrated by
John Meiczinger

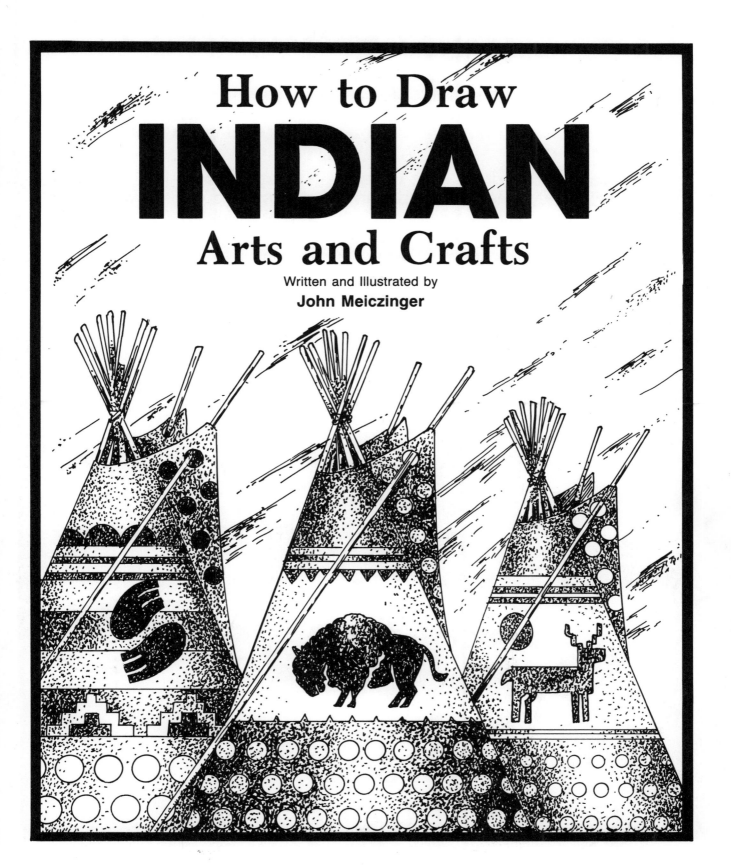

5513
Watermill Press

10   9   8   7   6   5   4   3   2   1   *Woodland Presbyterian School*

INTRODUCTION

Long before European settlers arrived in America, the North American Indians relied on their own skill and simple tools to create beautiful, well-crafted objects. They made homes, clothing, tools, weapons, cooking implements, and even ceremonial ornaments from the raw materials around them.

You can learn to draw these artifacts—it's easy, and it's fun! To begin, you will need some drawing paper; the size is up to you. It's also a good idea to have some tracing paper handy. This will allow you to practice by tracing over the drawings in this book. Be sure to have two #2 pencils and a kneaded eraser. A kneaded eraser won't leave fragments on your artwork as gum erasers do.

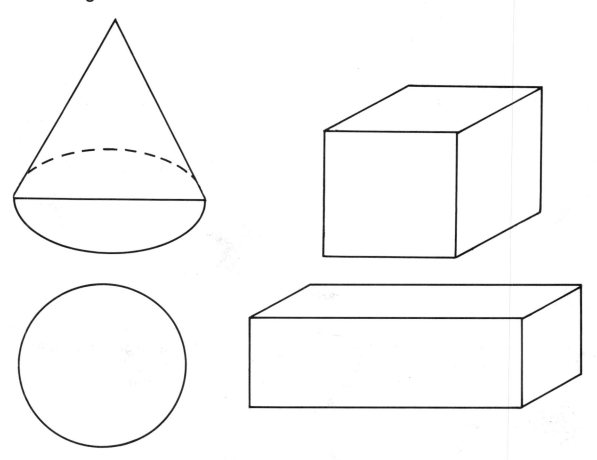

BASIC SHAPES

Most of the drawings in this book begin with these basic shapes. Draw the first steps lightly so that you can erase any unwanted lines. When your drawing looks the way you want it to, go over the pencil lines with black ink or a felt-tip marker. Then, color your Indian arts and crafts any way you like. Don't be afraid to be creative and, most of all, have fun!

TEPEES

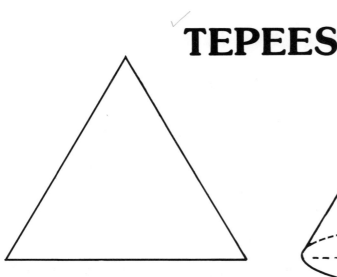

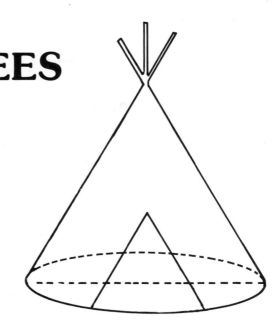

1. Begin your drawing with a triangle, and an oval shape.

2. Add a triangular shape for the door. Add poles at the top of the tepee, as shown. Erase dotted line.

3. Add the opening at the top of the tepee. Then, decorate your tepee any way you like.

NOTE: The Plains Indians tanned their buffalo hides to give them a lighter color. Then, they used the juices of berries as dyes to give their tepees a festive look.

The Plains Indians of the Midwest were nomadic hunters—always on the move. Their homes were made from twenty-foot (six-meter) poles that were covered by buffalo hides. These light, collapsible **tepees** could be put up and taken down quickly.

The poles were tied together at the top, forming a structure like an upside-down cone. The skins, which did not reach the point of the cone, left an open space through which smoke from cooking could pass.

WIGWAMS

Many Woodland Indians built homes called **wigwams** made of poles covered by tree bark. Dome-shaped wigwams, pictured below, were used as permanent shelter for families. Cone-shaped wigwams, such as those on page 5, were used as temporary shelter on hunting trips.

At the center of the wigwam was an open fire around which wooden platforms were set. The platforms, covered by animal skins or grass mats, were used for sitting and sleeping.

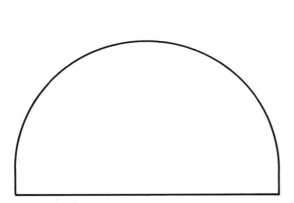

1. Start with a semicircle.

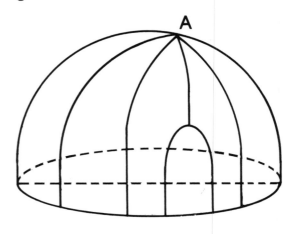

2. Draw an oval shape at the base. Then, beginning at fixed point A (slightly off center at the top of the circle), draw lines as shown to the bottom of the wigwam. Add a semi-oval shape for the door.

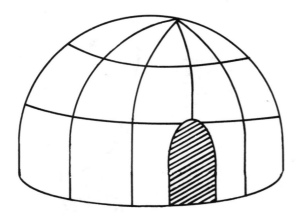

3. Add parallel lines across the width of the wigwam. Shade in your "door-way," using the side of your pencil point.

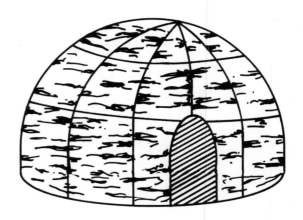

4. Again, use the side of your pencil point to add details that show the texture of the tree bark.

The temporary shelters of the Woodland Indians are much like the tepees of the Plains Indians (see page 3).

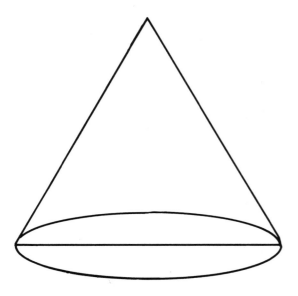

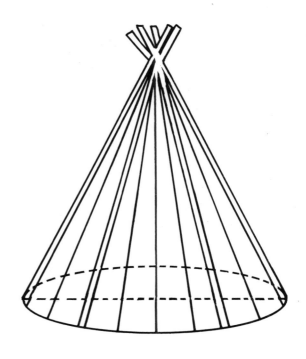

1. Start with a triangle and an oval shape.

2. Add lines, as shown, that extend to poles at the top of the wigwam. Erase dotted lines.

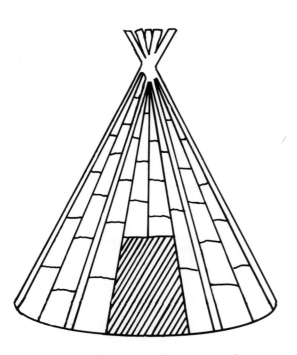

3. Small horizontal lines indicate that the wigwam is covered by tree bark. Add a "doorway" to the bottom-center of the wigwam; use the side of your pencil point to shade it in.

4. Again, use the side of your pencil point to add texture to your tree-bark shelter.

LONG HOUSES

The Iroquois Indians were known as "Five Nations," because they were actually five separate tribes. Also called "People of the **Long House**," the Iroquois lived in bark-covered homes that were often half as large as a football field. The length of the home was determined by the size of the family living in it.

Family members slept in bunk beds along the sides of the home. Food was cooked inside the long house over an open fire. Cooking smoke escaped through a hole in the roof of the house.

1. Start with a simple rectangle.

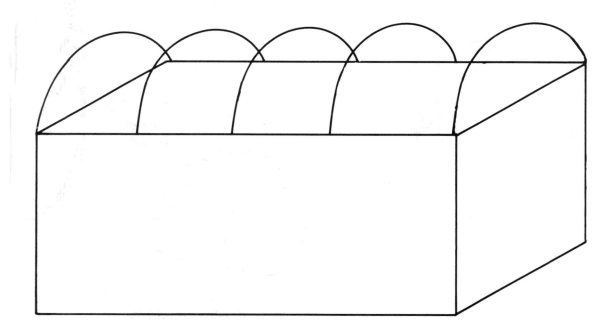

2. Give the rectangle dimension by adding lines, as shown. Now draw five semi-circular lines from the front of the rectangle to the back.

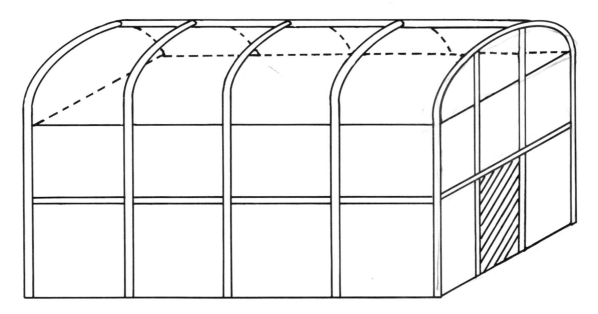

3. By rounding out the corners of your three-dimensional rectangle, you are shaping the top of your long house. Add parallel lines along the length and width, as shown. These lines represent the frame of the house, made from wooden poles. Add the "doorway," using the side of your pencil point for shading.

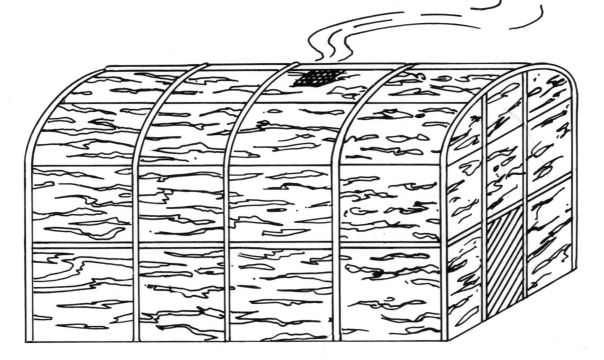

4. Again, use the side of your pencil point to add texture to your tree-bark long house.

FEATHERS

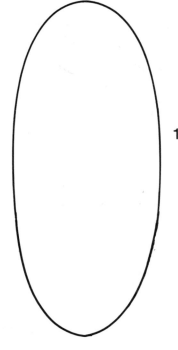

1. Draw an oval shape.

2. Taper the shape to a point, add a quill.

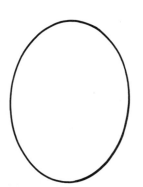

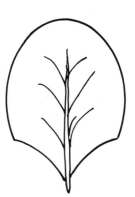

a. Draw a small oval.

b. Add a quill and details.

3. Give the feather a more realistic look by adding details, as shown.

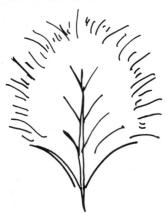

c. By making the lines on the edge of the feather you will create a "breath feather."

The down, or fluffy feathers at the base of the tail, were also used by the Indians. They were called "breath feathers," because the slightest breeze would make them look as though they were breathing.

FEATHER HEADDRESS

The Golden Eagle was a symbol of strength and courage to the American Indian. Its feathers were prized above all others as adornments in ceremonial **headdresses.** The thirteen tail feathers of the adult bird were also said to possess great medicine. These feathers are white with brown tips and measure 12 to 14 inches (30-35 centimeters) in length.

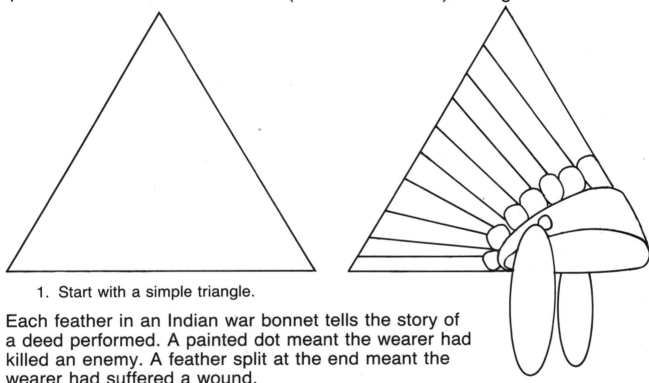

1. Start with a simple triangle.

Each feather in an Indian war bonnet tells the story of a deed performed. A painted dot meant the wearer had killed an enemy. A feather split at the end meant the wearer had suffered a wound.

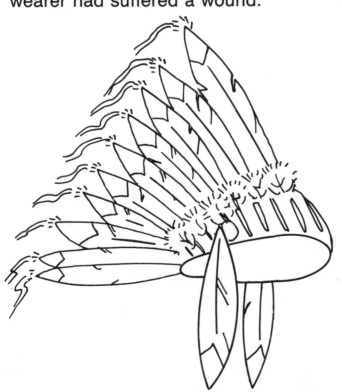

2. Add an oval in the lower right-hand corner, as shown. Shape the headband from the far right end of the oval to the left. Smaller oval shapes along the headband will be the base fluff feathers in Step 3. Lines extending from the ovals will be the larger eagle feathers. Add two elongated ovals, as shown; they will be the rosettes.

3. Shape your feathers. Add horsehair and other details. (Vertical lines along the headband are the binding.) Decorate your war bonnet anyway you like— perhaps, you can think of a story to go with it!

9

THE PEACE PIPE

The **peace pipe** was a sacred instrument used in religious, social, and political ceremonies. Decorations on the pipe and even the way it was held and passed on had significance. Smoking the peace pipe was a signal that the smoker gave a pledge of honor.

1. Start with a long rectangular shape for the stem of the pipe.

2. Add a small rectangle for the bowl of the pipe in which the tobacco was placed. Shape the opposite end of the pipe—that's the mouthpiece.

3. Add one small oval at the top of the bowl and several along the stem. These indentations in the stem of the pipe were helpful for gripping the object.

4. Add feathers and horsehair decoration. Now you're ready to "smoke" the peace pipe.

Most pipes were made of wood, clay, or stone with designs cut into them. Pipe stems were often decorated with feathers, horsehair, or colored cloth.

1. Start with a long, narrow rectangle.

2. Add the pipe's bowl and shape the mouthpiece, as shown. Add a triangular figure at the far left of the pipe. Decorate the stem and bowl of the pipe with straight, parallel lines. Add a shape at the bottom center, as shown, attached to the stem by small circles.

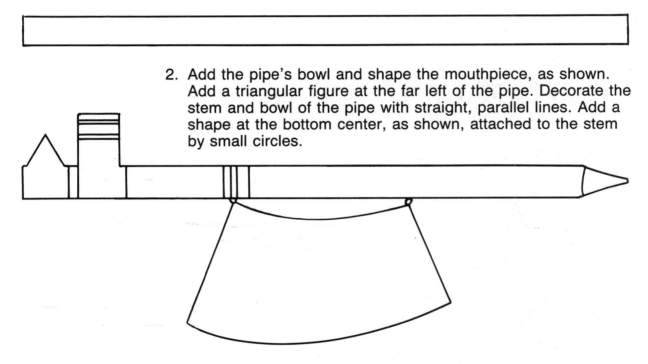

3. Complete the pipe by adding decorative items, such as those shown above: feathers, fringes, linear carvings along the stem and bowl. Finally, shape the triangular figure from the previous step into the head of an animal, such as the one shown above.

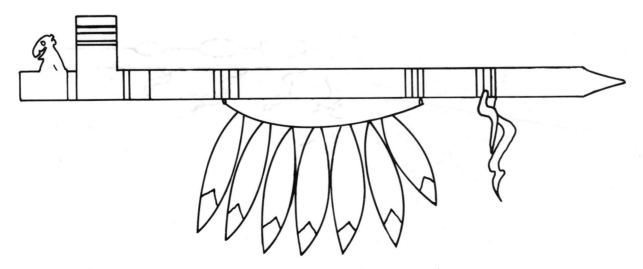

BOWS AND ARROWS

A well-designed and well-made **arrow** was important to Indian hunters. Each tribe had its own recognizable design. The arrow shafts were smooth and straight. The feathers at the base of the shaft were carefully trimmed. **Arrowheads** were either made of stone or of wood.

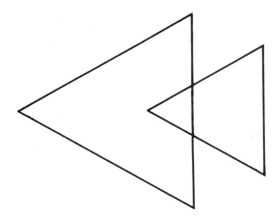

1. Start with two triangles, as shown.

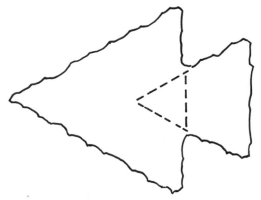

2. Shape the outer edges.

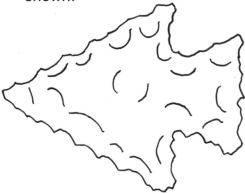

3. Draw the short curved lines to add more detail.

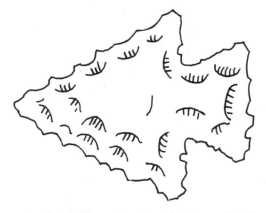

4. Add lines to give texture to the arrowhead.

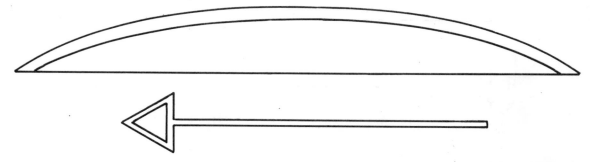

1. Start your **bow** with a long, straight line—that's the string for the arrow. Draw parallel lines that narrowly curve from the far left to the far right of the "string." The **arrow shaft** is a long wooden pole that is drawn with two parallel lines. The arrowhead is a small triangle at the end of the arrow shaft.

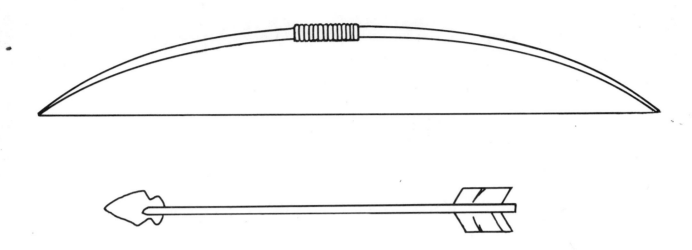

2. Add a small rectangle at the center of the bow—that's the grip with which the hunter held the bow and on which the arrow was positioned. Shape your arrowhead, as shown. Add feathers at the base of the shaft.

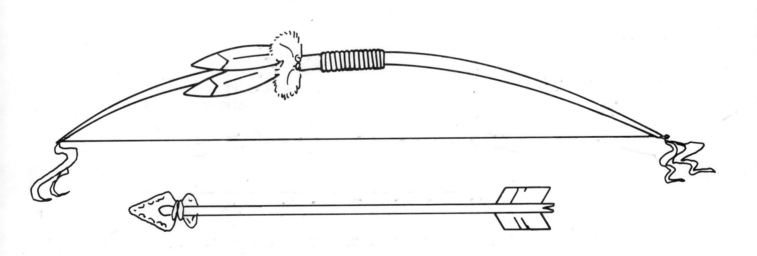

3. Decorative feathers, fluffs, and fringes were frequently placed on the bow. Add the decorations shown above, or make up a few of your own. Add details to the arrowhead. Add the binding that ties it to the shaft.

TOMAHAWKS

The **tomahawk** was a small ax used by the North American Indian as both a tool and a weapon. Most tomahawks were less than a foot and one half (45 centimeters) in length and were very lightweight. The head was usually made of stone mounted on a wooden handle.

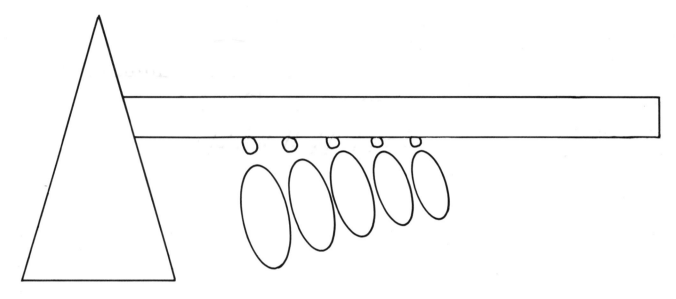

1. Start your drawing of a tomahawk with a triangle, a rectangle, several small ovals, and circles that will link them to the handle.

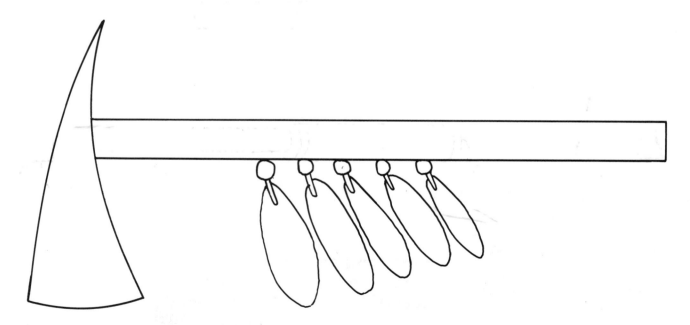

2. Shape the head of the tomahawk. Link the circles to the oval shapes. The ovals will become decorative feathers in the next step.

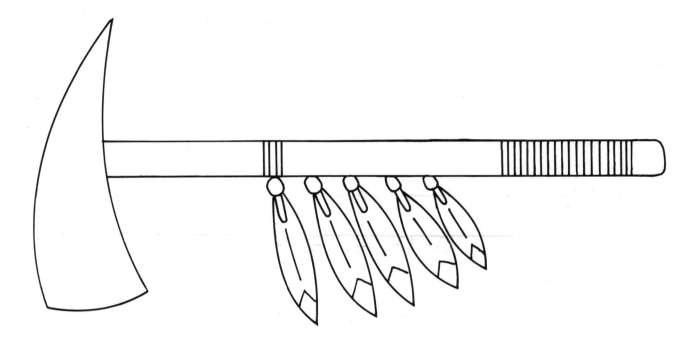

3. Decorate the feathers and the handle of the tomahawk.

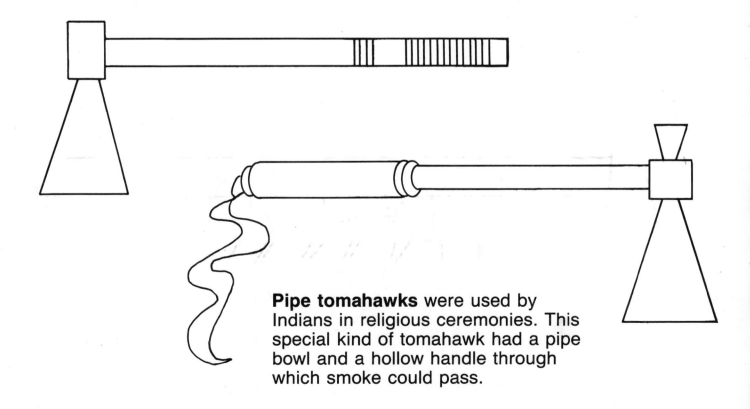

Pipe tomahawks were used by Indians in religious ceremonies. This special kind of tomahawk had a pipe bowl and a hollow handle through which smoke could pass.

CANOES

The Indians of North America made **canoes** to help them navigate rivers and streams. They were built by fastening bark to a wooden frame or by hollowing out a tree trunk.

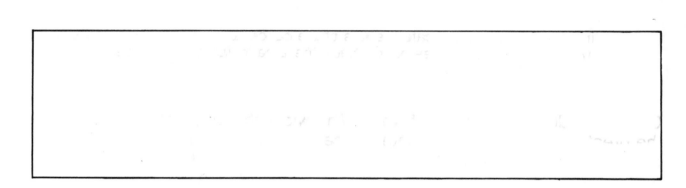

1. Start with a simple rectangular shape.

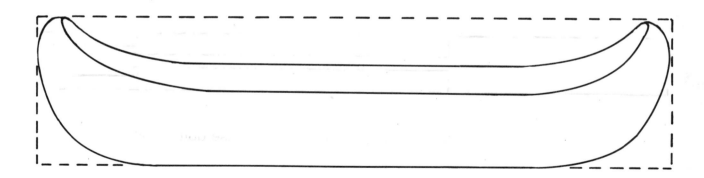

2. Extend two curved lines, as shown, from the upper left-hand corner to the right. Shape the curved outer edges, front and back, of the canoe. Erase dotted line.

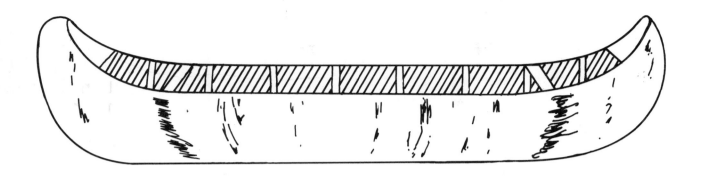

3. Add lines, as shown, to indicate the ribs of the canoe. Draw the lines on the side to show the texture of the tree bark. Shade the area inside of the canoe.

Canoe **paddles** were made of wood. The wider the blade of the paddle, the greater the power to navigate the canoe. Canoe paddles varied greatly in length, depending on the height of the user. (In general, canoe paddles should reach from the ground to eye level with the user.)

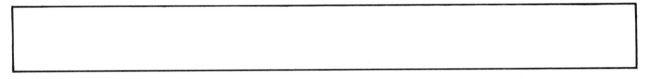

1. Start with a long, narrow rectangle.

2. Reduce the width of the pole and handle. Erase dotted line.

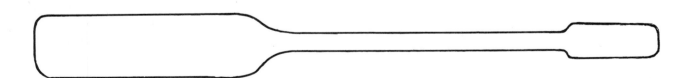

3. Shape the paddle's handle and blade.

TOBOGGAN

Indian hunters first built **toboggans** to carry buffalo hides over snow and ice. The toboggans were made of bark and were usually pulled by dogs.

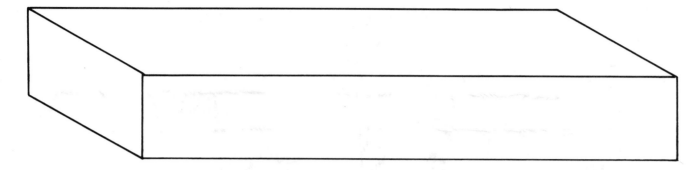

1. Start with a rectangle. Add lines to give it dimension.

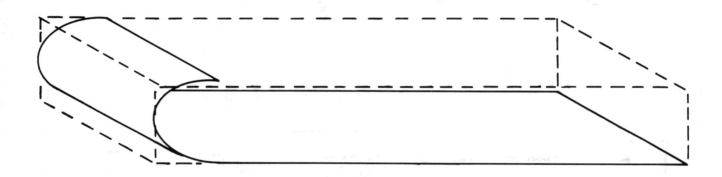

2. Curve the front end of the toboggan, as shown, erasing the rectangular guidelines.

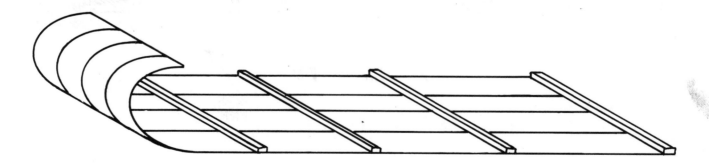

3. Add parallel lines to indicate strips of hickory, ash, or maple—the most common kinds of wood used to build toboggans. Finally, add the crosspieces used to fasten the strips together.

WAMPUM

Wampum was the American Indian word for beads made from shells. The beads were made by North American Indians in eastern coastal regions. Wampum was used to decorate clothing and to keep records of important events by arranging the beads in designs. White beads were carved from the shells of sea snails; purple beads were carved from hard-shell clams.

Fine holes were drilled in each bead so that they could be strung or sewn onto clothing. Wampum belts were then exchanged as pledges of peace and friendship. Later, they were used as **barter**, or money, in exchange for buffalo hides.

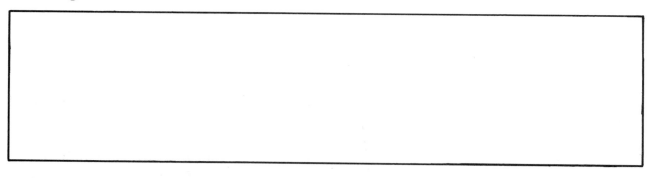

1. Start with a simple rectangle.

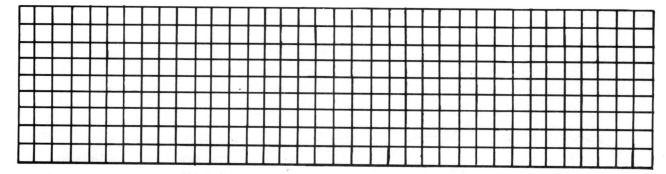

2. Form a grid inside the rectangle, as shown.

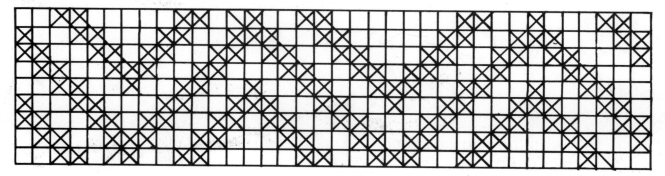

3. Create any design you like inside the grid—tell your own wampum story!

BUFFALO

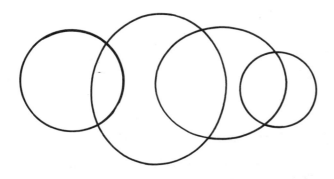

1. Begin your drawing of a buffalo with four interlocking circles.

2. Beginning with the buffalo's head at the left, shape the outline of the animal, as shown. Erase the dotted lines.

3. Add the ears, an eye, and the nose. Add details to indicate texture.

The buffalo was the source of most food, clothing, tools, housing, and cooking implements of the Plains Indians. Buffalo meat was either eaten fresh or preserved for later use. The skin of the buffalo was used for clothing, footwear, bedding, and the outer coverings of tepees. It took twenty or more hides sewn together to make one tepee covering.

BASKETS

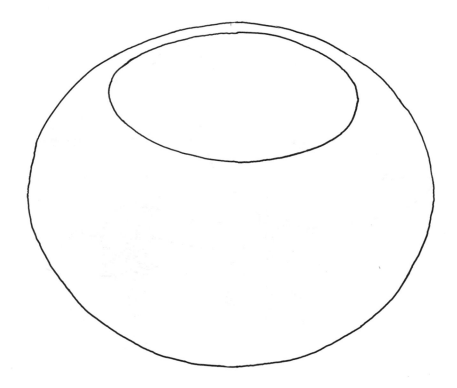

1. Start with a circle. Add a smaller-sized oval at the top center of the circle.

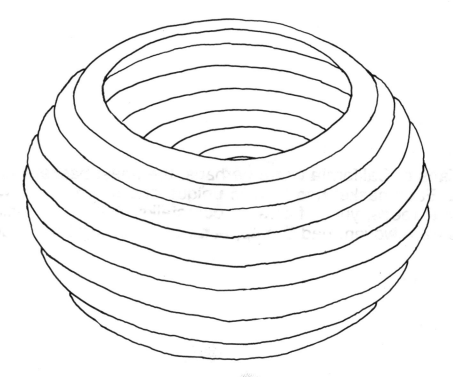

2. Add concentric circles, as shown, to begin the "weave" of your basket.

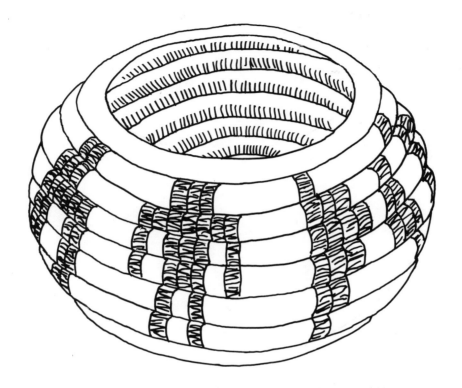

3. Add smaller lines for texture. Now draw your own special basket design, or copy the one above.

The Indians of California were, perhaps, the finest basket weavers in America. Each basket had its own unique design whether it was woven from cattail reeds, yucca fibers, or cornstalks. Some, into which small feathers were woven, had the appearance of having been studded with jewels.

POTTERY

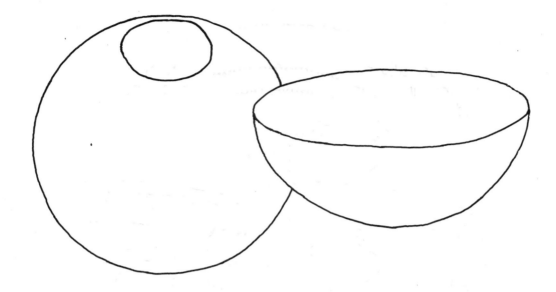

1. Start your drawing of the vase with a circle. Add a small-sized oval at the top center. Begin your bowl with a long, narrow oval placed in a horizontal position. Extend a curved line from the far left to the far right corner of the oval.

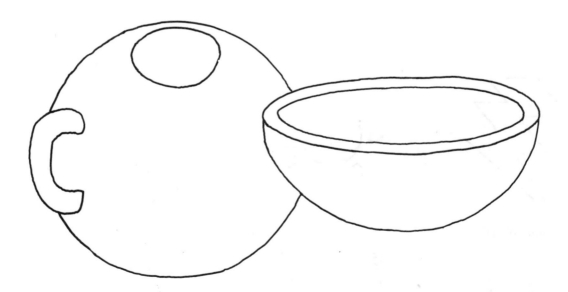

2. Add a handle to the vase and a rim to the bowl, as shown.

The Indians of the Southwest were peaceable farmers and had a permanent, stable society. These skilled craftspeople often used clay to make jars, pots, bowls, and other items. The crafts were shaped by hand, dried in the sun, and then decorated with paints made from earth and minerals. Finally, the pottery was baked in a large, dome-shaped oven called a kiln.

The Pueblo Indians usually put geometric shapes on their pottery for decoration. But, sometimes, imaginative pictures of plants or animals were used instead.

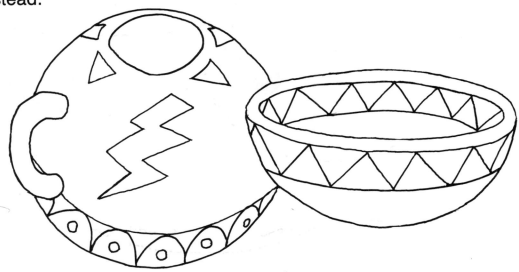

3. Now decorate both your vase and your bowl. You may use the suggested symbols below, or make up designs of your own.

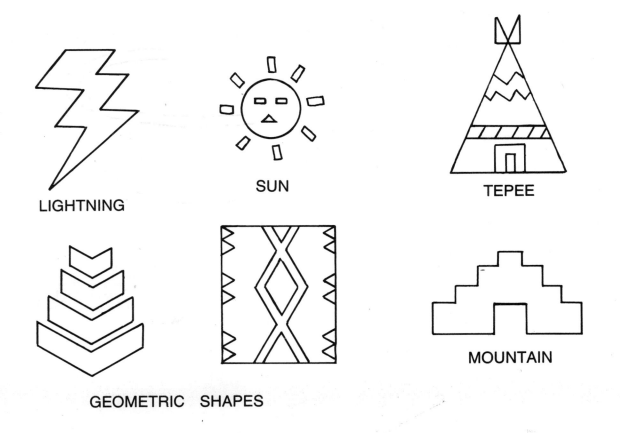

LIGHTNING

SUN

TEPEE

MOUNTAIN

GEOMETRIC SHAPES

TOTEM POLES

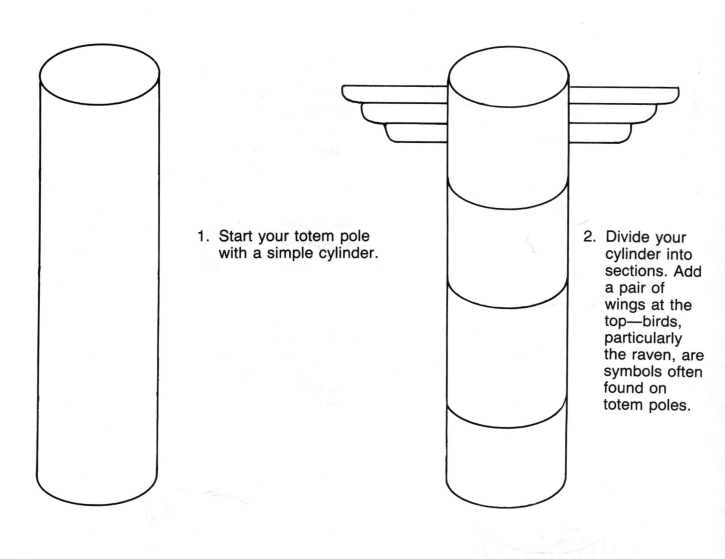

1. Start your totem pole with a simple cylinder.

2. Divide your cylinder into sections. Add a pair of wings at the top—birds, particularly the raven, are symbols often found on totem poles.

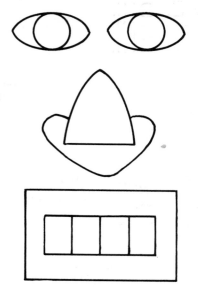

3. The designs above can be used to help you draw the figures on the totem pole.

The Indians of the Pacific Northwest were noted for large wood carvings known as **totem poles**. These carved cedar poles were originally used as corner posts for Indian homes. Later, it became the custom to erect a totem pole in front of the house. Totems told the story of the owner's family history, or of a brave deed accomplished. Some were memorials to the dead. Others told of mythological adventures.

4. Now decorate your totem pole any way you like. You may use the designs suggested below, or make up a few of your own. Have your totem pole tell a story, just like those of the Northwest Indians.

Here are some of the figures that were common to the **totem poles** of the Pacific Northwest.

MASKS

Masks were often used in religious ceremonies or in dancing—just for fun! The mask below is a "wildman" mask. It tells the story of a man who loses his wits when he's bitten by an animal.

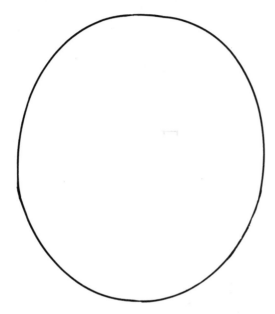

1. Start with an oval shape.

2. Add the eyes, nose, and mouth. Additional lines, as shown, give expression to the face.

3. Add details to the eyes, nose, and mouth. Use the lines from the previous step as guidelines for creating the eyebrows as well as details around the chin and the cheeks. Add lines for hair at the top of the mask—stop here if it's getting too scary!

4. For an even more gruesome wildman mask, add the details shown above.

The mask on this page was worn on ceremonial occasions by the Indian chief. The sections rising from the top of the hat show the chief's rank within the tribe, just as a sergeant's stripes indicate his position in the armed forces.

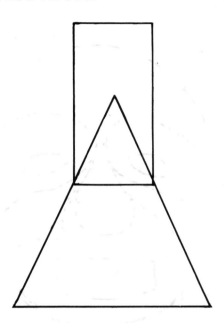

1. Start with a triangular shape interlocking with a simple rectangle.

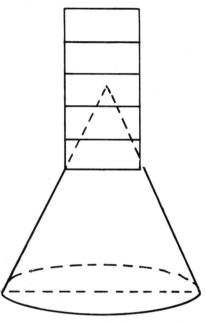

2. Subdivide the rectangle, as shown. Shape the bottom of the triangle into a cone.

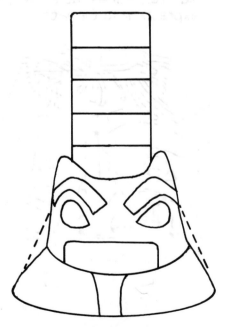

3. Soften the contours of the "cone" along the top and bottom. Add details to the mask face.

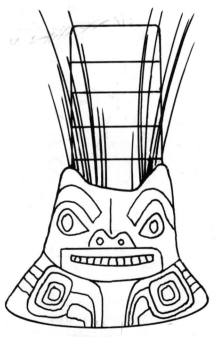

4. Decorate your mask, as shown above, or anyway you like. The hair extending from the top of the mask was probably made of grass or reeds.

KACHINA DOLL

The Pueblo people believed that **kachinas** were intermediaries between man and god. They were thought to bring good things such as rain, crops, sunlight, and long life. Kachina dolls represented these supernatural beings.

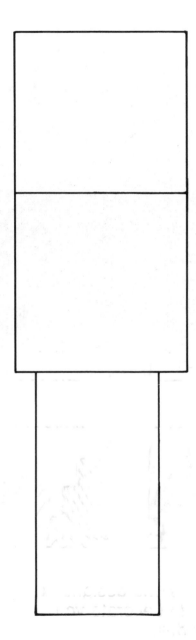

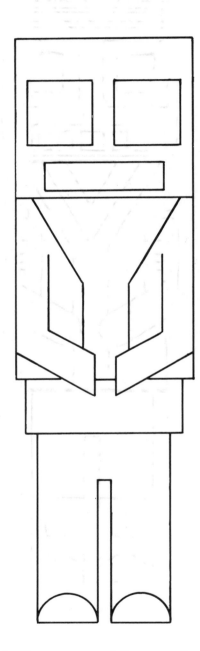

1. Start your kachina doll with two squares and a long rectangle below them. The squares will be the head and the body; the rectangle will be the legs.

2. Fill in the eyes and the mouth; the arms and the jacket; the legs and the feet.

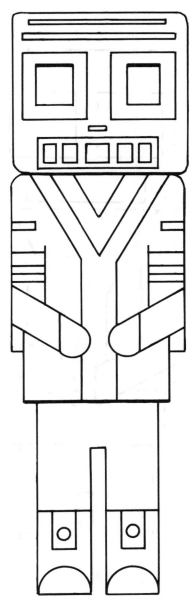

3. Then, decorate your kachina doll anyway you like, or follow the suggested kachina doll pattern to the left. Perhaps, this kachina brings sunlight—note the sun above its head.

Here are some designs you can use to decorate your kachina doll.

CORN

When European settlers first arrived in the New World, they were taught how to plant and grow corn. Known to the Native Americans as maize, corn has become symbolic of the harmony between the European and the Indian cultures.

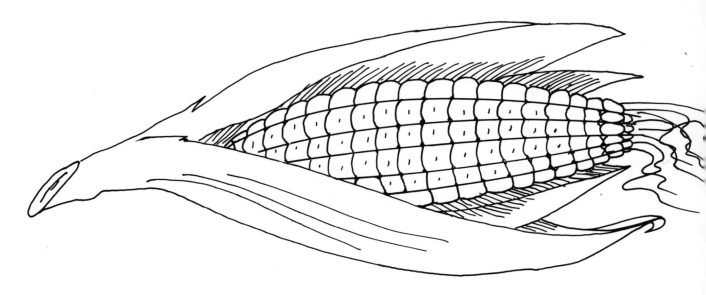

Use the basic shapes and techniques you have learned in this book to draw an ear of corn. Perhaps, you can put it at the center of a cornucopia you draw yourself!